MW01153039

PRIMARY HANDBOOK FOR MALLETS

A Beginning Method with Play-Along Audio

by GARWOOD WHALEY

PLAYBACK+
Speed • Pitch • Balance • Loop

To access audio visit:
www.halleonard.com/mylibrary

Enter Code
2716-4416-6844-7420

International Standard Book Number: 978-0-634-03924-9
Printed and bound in U.S.A.

MEREDITH MUSIC PUBLICATIONS and its stylized double M logo are trademarks
of MEREDITH MUSIC PUBLICATIONS, a division of G.W. Music, Inc.

MEREDITH MUSIC PUBLICATIONS
a division of G.W. Music, Inc.
4899 Lerch Creek Ct., Galesville, MD 20765
http://www.meredithmusic.com

EXCLUSIVELY DISTRIBUTED BY

7777 W. BLUEMOUND RD. P.O. BOX 13819 MILWAUKEE, WI 53213

FOREWORD

The purpose of this text is to provide a comprehensive course of study for the beginning mallet/keyboard percussion student. This volume contains all of the fundamental elements of mallet playing. Included are technical studies, tunes for memorization, reading studies, four-mallet studies for beginning technical development, student composition assignments and an introduction to ensemble performance through the use of duets. All studies are based on a variety of materials that include major and minor keys, a varied use of time signatures, simple to intricate rhythmic combinations, marks of expression and tempi and musical styles ranging from Baroque to Jazz. Student composition assignments provide a unique introduction to musical creativity. Each assignment is designed to increase the student's comprehensive musical knowledge as outlined in the National Standards for Arts Education.

By consistent and intelligent practice of these materials, the student's improvement will be rapid. I sincerely hope that this volume provides an enjoyable approach to mallet/keyboard percussion playing.

G.W.

PREFACE

PRIMARY HANDBOOK FOR MALLETS is designed to provide the beginning mallet/keyboard percussion student with a complete course of studies utilizing both major and minor keys. Each set of two pages focuses on a specific key and contains a variety of studies. Included in this volume are:

TECHNICAL EXERCISES – Fundamental technical exercises appear in twelve major and six minor keys. One octave scales, triads, chromatic scales and third studies provide a basic technical foundation. Each technical study should be memorized and practiced repeatedly.

READINGS STUDIES – Reading studies progress in complexity and in the use of musical terminology and marks of expression. Each study utilizes specific rhythmic combinations, compositional devices, styles, key signatures and time signatures. Students should be encouraged to look at (focus on) the music and, using peripheral vision, the keyboard when reading. These studies should not be memorized.

4 MALLET STUDIES – The 4 mallet studies presented in this book were designed to introduce a technique that has become standard for today's keyboard percussionist. Each study should be memorized so that the student can focus on accurate placement of each mallet.

MEMORIZATION – Memorizing familiar and progressively less familiar melodies will help to develop the ability to memorize music and visually learn the arrangement of pitches on the keyboard. Looking at the printed music and 'seeing" each note in your mind is an excellent method of memorizing before actually playing.

STUDENT COMPOSITION ASSIGNMENTS – An understanding of the creative process of composition is necessary in order to become a complete musician. The composition assignments are designed to provide an introduction to this process through the introduction of standard compositional devices. Each exercise should be carefully prepared and performed.

DUETS – The duets contained in this text provide students with pre-ensemble performance experience. Both parts of each duet should be prepared.

PRACTICE CHARTS – To reinforce the need for consistent study, a practice chart is provided at the bottom of each page. Students should be encouraged to record their practice time daily. Requesting parents to sign the practice chart can provide additional reinforcement.

AUDIO – The audio provides an excellent aural model for the Reading Studies, 4 Mallet Studies, Memorization and Duets. Try playing each study before listening to the recording, then listen to the audio and compare your playing with the recording. You may also play along with the audio to improve your ability to play at a steady tempo and to keep playing without stopping. One full measure of clicks precedes most examples. To access the audio, go to **www.halleonard.com/mylibrary** and enter the code found on page 1.

TEMPO MARKS – Tempo marks are provided as a guide only. Producing an even, musical sound with consistent tone quality is the first priority in developing musicianship.

PERFORMANCE FUNDAMENTALS

STICKING – Generally, all strokes on mallet instruments are alternated (LRLR or RLRL). To eliminate cross sticking ascending passages usually begin with the left hand and descending passages with the right. Doubling (repeating a stroke with the same hand) should be avoided unless it provides a technical means of playing an otherwise difficul passage or a desired phrasing.

ROLL – A roll is used to sustain one or more pitches. It is notated with three horizontal slashes above the notehead and produced by alternating single strokes. The single strokes should be even and need only be moderately fast. Strive to produce a smooth, continuous sound.

POSTURE AND POSITION – Assume a relaxed yet well supported position approximately six inches from the instrumen and directly behind the area on which you are playing. The forearms should be approximately parallel with the ground (if the height of the instrument will not permit this, an adjustment must be made to raise or lower the instrument).

PLAYING AREA – Each bar must be struck in the correct area in order to produce a full, resonant sound. Use a full relaxed down-up stroke. Strike the accidental bars on the end closest to the performer and the natural bars in the middle. Never strike a bar over the connecting cord.

GLOSSARY

Tempo

Agitato - agitated, excited
Alla Marcia - in march style
Allegretto - moderately fast
Allegro - lively, rapid
Allegro Assai - very fast
Allegro Moderato - moderately fast
Andante - moderately slow, flowing
Brillante - brilliant, showy
Energico - energetically
Largo - very slow
Maestoso - majestic, dignified
Moderato - moderately
Presto - fast (faster than Allegro)
Risoluto - resolute, bold
Ritardando (rit.) - a gradual slowing of tempo
Scherzando - playfully
Vivace - lively, brisk
Vivo - lively, spirited

Expression

Pianissimo (*pp*) - very soft
Piano (*p*) - soft
Mezzo forte (*mf*) - moderately loud
Forte (*f*) - loud
Fortissimo (*ff*) - very loud
Sempre - always
Espressive (esp.) - with expression
Crescendo ⎯⎯⎯⎯ - gradually louder
Decrescendo ⎯⎯⎯⎯ - gradually softer

Repeats

D.C. al fine - repeat to the beginning and play to the end (Fine).

D.S. al fine - repeat to the sign (𝄋) and play to the end (Fine).

CLEF – Music for keyboard percussion instruments is usually written in the treble or G clef. Memorize the following clef and all notes including those using leger lines above and below the staff.

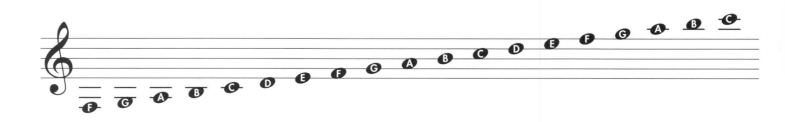

HAND POSITION

Two Mallets: Both mallets are held alike when playing with two mallets.

Turn the palm of the hand up. Hold the mallet between the fleshy part of the thumb and the first joint of the index finger. Wrap the last three fingers wrap around the end of the mallet shaft (fig. 1).Turn the palm of the hand down. Remember to hold the mallets with a firm but relaxed grip. Compare your hand position with that of the diagram (fig. 2).

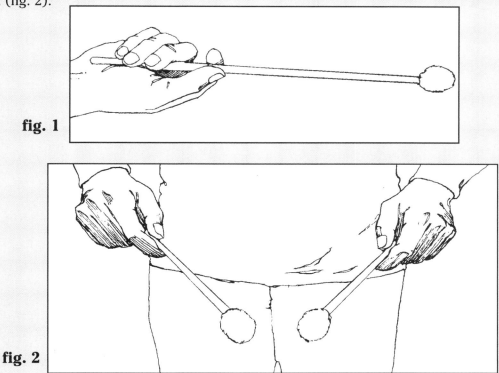

fig. 1

fig. 2

Four Mallets: The Musser Grip — one of several standard four mallet grips — allows a great deal of flexibility and independence. The mallets in both the right and left hands are held alike.

Turn the palm of the hand up. Hold the inside mallet beneath the third finger and between the fleshy part of the thumb and the first joint of the index finger. Hold the outside mallet beneath the fourth and fifth fingers. Do not allow this mallet to extend beyond the end of the hand (fig. 3). Turn the palm of the hand down. Remember to hold the mallets with a firm but relaxed grip. Compare your hand position with that of the diagram (fig. 4).

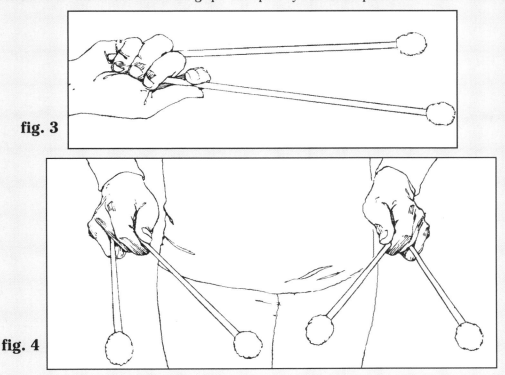

fig. 3

fig. 4

C Major

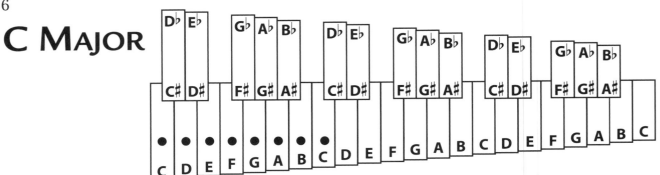

Technical Exercises

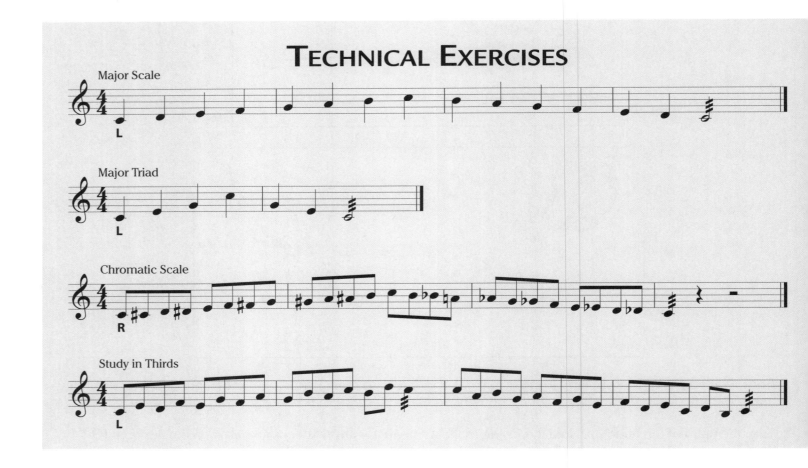

Major Scale

Major Triad

Chromatic Scale

Study in Thirds

Reading Study 1

♩ = 80-92

Count: 1 2 3 4 1 2 3 4

1 2 3 4

	Lesson Day	1	2	3	4	5	6		Total Time
Record your practice time for each day of the week.								=	

4 MALLET STUDY

MEMORIZATION
My Darlin' Clementine

Montrose

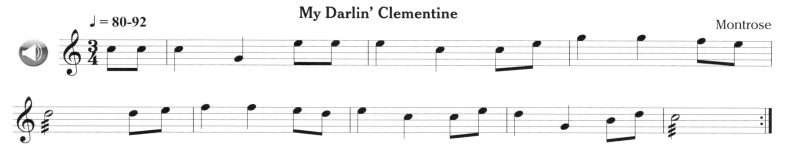

READING STUDY 2

STUDENT COMPOSITION ASSIGNMENT

Complete (and play) the following by writing the original two measures in reverse —
this is a compositional device called *retrograde*.

	Lesson Day	1	2	3	4	5	6		Total Time
Record your practice time for each day of the week.								=	

4 MALLET STUDY

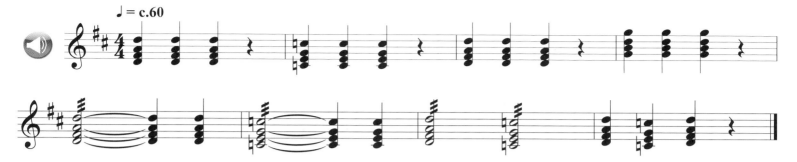

MEMORIZATION

The Marines Hymm
(from the opera *The Grand Duchess*)

Offenbach

READING STUDY 10

STUDENT COMPOSITION ASSIGNMENT

Complete (and play) the following by repeating the original two measures beginning on a different scale degree — this is called a *sequence*.

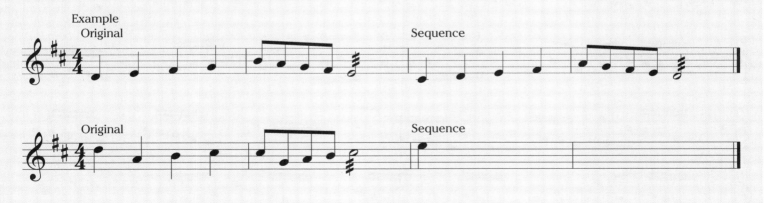

	Lesson Day	1	2	3	4	5	6		Total Time
Record your practice time for each day of the week.								=	

16

E♭ MAJOR

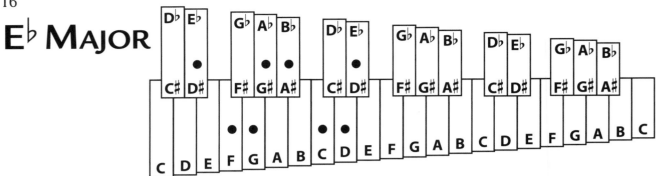

TECHNICAL EXERCISES

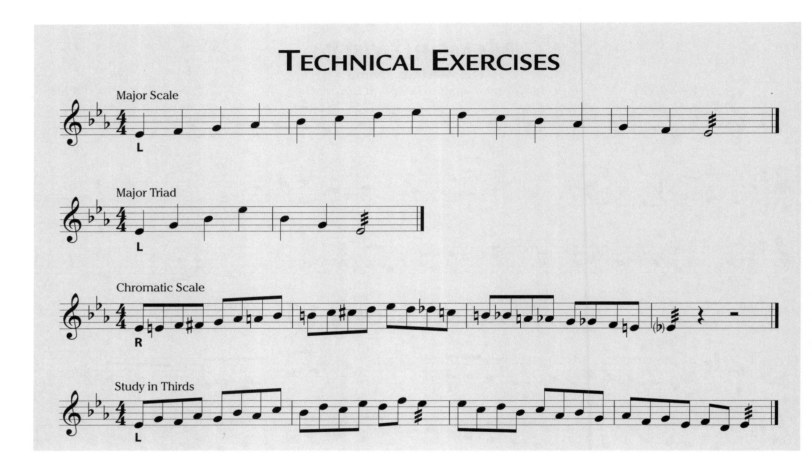

Major Scale

Major Triad

Chromatic Scale

Study in Thirds

READING STUDY 11

Moderato ♩ = 50-72

Count: **1 e & a 2** **3 e & a 4**

1 e & a 2 **&** **3 e & a 4** **&**

	Lesson Day	1	2	3	4	5	6	Total Time
Record your practice time for each day of the week.								=

4 MALLET STUDY

MEMORIZATION

William Tell Overture

Rossini

READING STUDY 12

STUDENT COMPOSITION ASSIGNMENT

Transpose (and play) the *William Tell Overture* exerpt in the key of C major.

Lesson Day	1	2	3	4	5	6		Total Time

Record your practice time for each day of the week.

A MAJOR

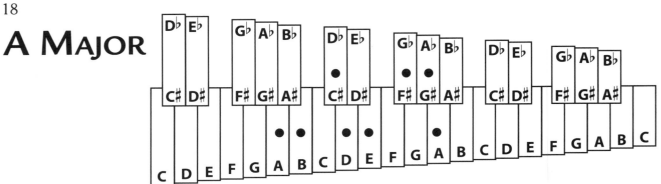

TECHNICAL EXERCISES

READING STUDY 13

Record your practice time for each day of the week.

Lesson Day	1	2	3	4	5	6	Total Time

4 Mallet Study

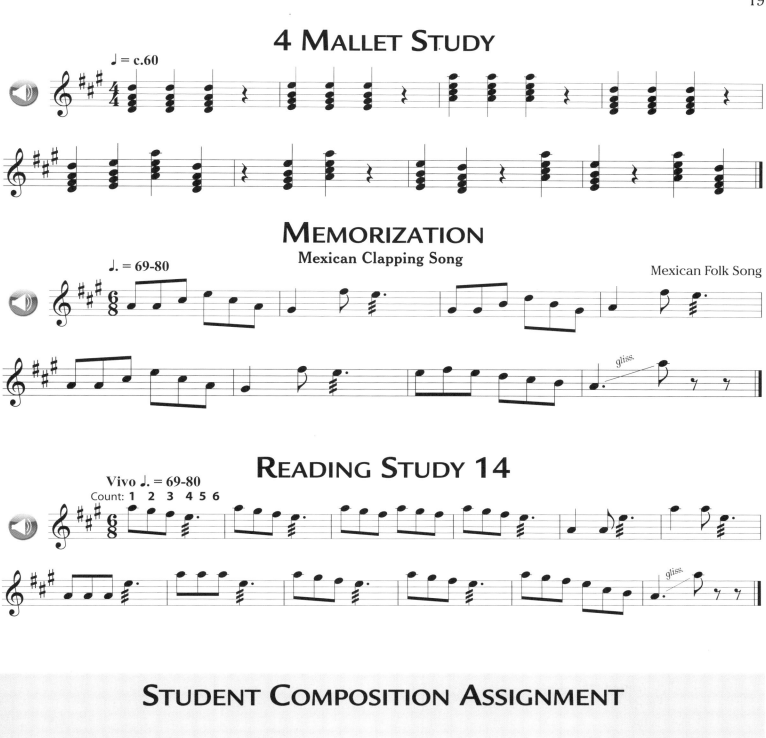

Memorization
Mexican Clapping Song

Mexican Folk Song

Reading Study 14

Student Composition Assignment

Write (and play) the following in *retrograde* (see page 7).

Lesson Day	1	2	3	4	5	6		Total Time
Record your practice time for each day of the week.							=	

4 MALLET STUDY

MEMORIZATION

Turkey In The Straw

Traditional

READING STUDY 24

STUDENT COMPOSITION ASSIGNMENT

Transpose (and play) the first eight measures of *Turkey In The Straw* in the key of F major.

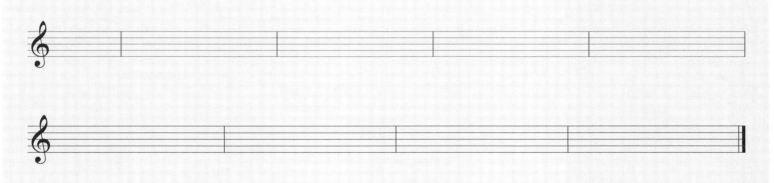

Record your practice time for each day of the week.

Lesson Day	1	2	3	4	5	6		Total Time
							=	

A MINOR

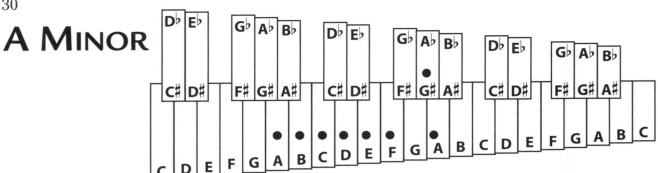

TECHNICAL EXERCISES

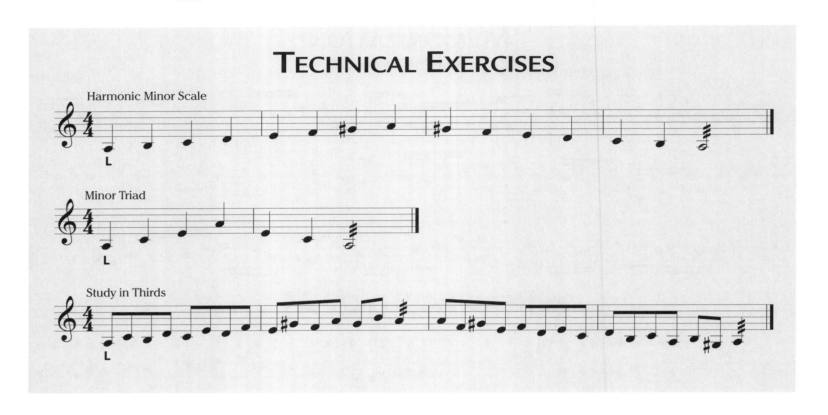

Harmonic Minor Scale

Minor Triad

Study in Thirds

READING STUDY 25

Adagio ♩ = 66-76

	Lesson Day	1	2	3	4	5	6		Total Time

Record your practice time for each day of the week.

4 MALLET STUDY

♩ = c.60

4 3 2 1 1 2 3 4

MEMORIZATION

When Johnny Comes Marching Home

Lambert

♩. = 100-112

READING STUDY 26

Vivace ♪ = 190-200

STUDENT COMPOSITION ASSIGNMENT

Rewrite (and play) the first eight measures of *Irish Washerwoman* (page 27) using *diminution* — the halving of note values.

Example
Original

Diminution

	Lesson Day	1	2	3	4	5	6		Total Time
Record your practice time for each day of the week.								=	

D MINOR

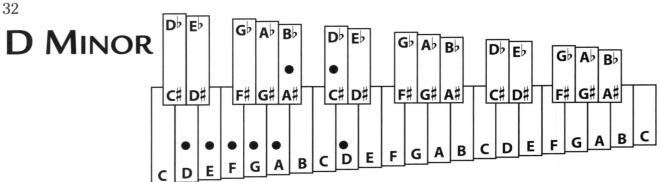

TECHNICAL EXERCISES

Harmonic Minor Scale

Minor Triad

Study in Thirds

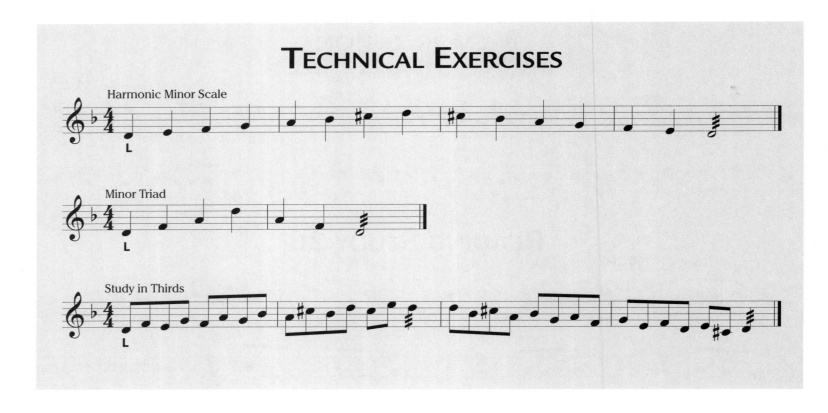

READING STUDY 27

Allegro moderato ♩ = 66-76

mf sempre

rit.

	Lesson Day	1	2	3	4	5	6		Total Time
Record your practice time for each day of the week.								=	

4 MALLET STUDY

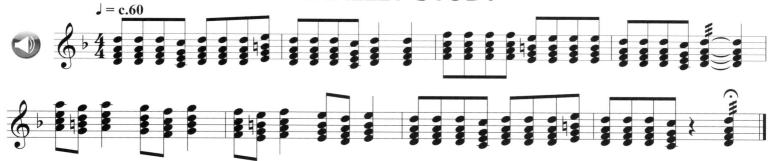

MEMORIZATION

Waltz

Schubert

READING STUDY 28

STUDENT COMPOSITION ASSIGNMENT

Transpose (and play) the first eight measures of Schubert's *Waltz* to D major.

	Lesson Day	1	2	3	4	5	6		Total Time

Record your practice time for each day of the week.

DUET 2

(Menuet)

J. S. Bach

DUET 3
(Gigue)

Boismortier

Duet 4

Telemann

Duet 5
(Polonaise)

J. S. Bach

DUET 6
(Allegro from Sonata VI, Op. 5)

Quantz